# I Can Take A Shower

Written by Chemise Taylor

Illustrated by Alexis B. Taylor

Copyright © 2019 by My Skills Books

Published by My Skills Books

All rights reserved. No part of this publication may be reproduced, distributed, or transmitted in any form or by any means, including photocopying, recording, or other electronic or mechanical methods, without the prior written permission of the publisher, except in the case of brief quotations embodied in critical reviews and certain other noncommercial uses permitted by copyright law.

First Printing, 2019.


ISBN: 978-1-951573-06-5

www.myskillsbooks.com

I'm smelly and sweaty, but I had so much fun.
Today was the day my team actually won.

I come inside after a hard day of play and my mom says....

"Go take a shower, right away."

Okay! No problem, at all. I go and turn the shower faucet on.

**Once the temperature is right, I jump on in. The water feels great on my skin.**

I grab my body wash and loofah, too. One to two squirts should do.

I use the loofah to wash my skin.

# I wash my....

| | |
|---|---|
| arms | chest |
| tummy | back |
| legs | behind |
| neck | underarms |
| feet | toes |

and private area

Now, it's time to wash my hair. I grab my shampoo and give it a squeeze.

One to two squirts in my hand, is all I need.

I rub the shampoo on my scalp and try not to get any in my eyes.  As the shampoo lathers, the bubbles rise and rise.

After I'm done washing my hair, I stand under the water and rinse out all the shampoo. I rinse the soap off of my body too.

I turn off the faucet until there is no more water. Now it is time for me to get out of the shower.

I grab my dirty clothes, as I leave the bathroom.  I'll put them in the laundry hamper that is in my bedroom.

I go to my bedroom and find clean pajamas to wear. I wrap the towel around my head, to help dry my hair.

**All done! Hey mom, look at me!
I am now fresh and clean.**

# Book Details

**Story Word Count:** 248

**Key Words:** Shower, Wash, Soap, Shampoo, Towel, Lather, Hair, Body

**Comprehension Check**

- What was the story about?
- What did she wash her body with?
- What did she wash her hair with?

# Reading Award

This certificate goes to:

_____

for reading "I Can Take A Shower"

## Good Job!

More books, apps and resources at myskillsbooks.com

www.ingramcontent.com/pod-product-compliance
Lightning Source LLC
Chambersburg PA
CBHW040051130526

44591CB00029B/48